About Us

Absolute Crime publishes only the best true crime literature. Our focus is on the crimes that you've probably never heard of, but you are fascinated to read more about. With each engaging and gripping story, we try to let readers relive moments in history that some people have tried to forget.

Remember, our books are not meant for the faint at heart. We don't hold back — if a crime is bloody, we let the words splatter across the page so you can experience the crime in the most horrifying way!

If you enjoy this book, please visit our homepage to see other books we offer; if you have any feedback, we'd love to hear from you!

The Holdouts

The Imperial Japanese Army deployed hundreds of thousands of Japanese soldiers across Asia during World War II, from the cold northern steppes of Manchuria to the sweltering islands of the South Pacific. Fascist and militarist leaders in Tokyo sought to carve out a vast domain for Japan, which was an emergent world power long before Pearl Harbor. Farmers' sons had become Japan's infantrymen, taught that Japan was divine, invincible and destined to rule all Asia. By 1910, Japan had soldiers in Korea, Taiwan, and Beijing. In the 1930s, the Japanese Army took Manchuria, rich with the mineral resources to fuel Japan's industrial and imperial growth, and entered China in force. By the time Japan officially entered World War II in December 1941, the Imperial Japanese Army was spread across Asia. The vast distance between Japan and America made direct confrontation impossible. Neither side had a foothold close enough to attack the other. The war between America and Japan had to take place in the South Pacific islands, tiny points of land separated by hundreds of miles of ocean. The Japanese Army spread itself thin to protect this artery, the gateway to the home islands.

Japanese soldiers were stationed on islands across the Southwest Pacific, with names exotic and yet familiar: Guam, Guadalcanal, Saipan, Lubang and Peleliu. As the Allied island-hopping campaign encircled Japan, thousands of Japanese soldiers were cut off from their command and were presumed killed-in-action. One by one, Japan's island fortresses fell to the Americans. Many Japanese soldiers chose to die in futile banzai attacks to retake what they had lost. Faced with a desperate decision between dying in suicidal charges and going into hiding, most Japanese soldiers chose suicide. Surrender was anathema to soldiers of the Imperial Japanese Army: it was considered a grave dishonor and was punishable by death under the military codes of conduct. To a man, Japanese soldiers were taught to prefer death over capture or defeat. Even to retreat was considered a disgrace. Rather than fall back and reform, to attempt to restore communications with their superiors, countless Japanese infantrymen on dozens of islands across the Pacific chose to die in last-ditch, banzai attacks on the enemy. To die gloriously in battle was preferable to them than the shame of defeat or capture. It was a desperate choice.

The holdouts, on the other hand, chose to live, even if that meant suffering deprivation, hardship and shame. However strange the stragglers may seem for their decision to run and hide — sometimes for decades — it was either that or to die "honorably." Many stragglers were burdened with survivor's guilt and felt immense shame that they had not died in battle with their comrades. Their sense of guilt was so great that some preferred to endure decades of hunger, exposure and isolation rather than face their countrymen again.

Most of the holdouts gradually emerged from hiding during the late 1940s and 1950s. In the chaos of the final months of the war tens of thousands of Japanese soldiers were abandoned at remote outposts in the Pacific Islands and Manchuria.

A few holdouts — the most famous of the lot — only came down from the mountains ten to thirty years after the war. Each had their own reasons for refusing to surrender, but the longest-running holdouts had a lot in common. They were all hopelessly cut off from their commanders and had no way of knowing how the war was going. When stranded Japanese soldiers found out the war was over through the proper channels, they usually surrendered. Some soldiers were so isolated and so far from any trusted source of information about the war that they were left to imagine the worst and hope for the best. Military indoctrination had taught Japanese soldiers that their country was invincible, and in the absence of evidence to the contrary, most assumed that the war was still ongoing. Ignorance kept them from surrendering more than anything else.

Some stragglers, like Sergeant Shoichi Yokoi, one of only a handful of Japanese survivors of the Second Battle of Guam, knew that Japan had lost the war but nevertheless stayed in hiding for 28 years. Many holdouts believed they would be killed, either by the Allies or by islanders seeking revenge for Japan's wartime atrocities. American Marines hunted down Japanese survivors in relentless search-and-destroy missions: those who did not surrender immediately were killed. Those who survived the search-and-destroy missions were often traumatized and fearful of surrender. Why then did some holdouts stay hidden even years after the Americans had left?

They stayed hidden because they were sincerely afraid of being looked down upon if they returned to Japan. And their fear was sometimes justified. A few stragglers even received letters urging them to commit suicide to atone for their supposed disgrace. Yokoi summed up how many stragglers felt when he famously said in 1972, "It is with much embarrassment, but I have returned."

Still other holdouts, like Teruo Nakamura, the last Japanese holdout to emerge from hiding in 1974, firmly believed that Japan had won, or at the very least, was still fighting. Nakamura was stranded on Morotai in late 1944 after the Allies retook the island in preparation for an assault on the Philippines. He was declared dead in March 1945. For the next thirty years, he grew his own food, raised fowl, hunted wild boar, and lived in a small thatched hut deep in the mountain jungles of Morotai. He would occasionally trade with the islanders, who tried to explain to him many times that the war was over and Japan had been defeated. Nakamura simply refused to believe them. "Japan is invincible," he would say. It wasn't until the Indonesian government learned of his presence and sent out a search party to arrest him that Nakamura left Morotai.

Nakamura was not the only holdout who thought Japan could never be defeated. Lt. Hiro Onoda held out on the island of Lubang for almost as long as Nakamura: from 1945 to 1974. For thirty years Onoda waged a one-man "guerrilla war" on Lubang—meaning he occasionally stole food and supplies from the Lubang islanders, and killed many of them in the process. Onoda was a true holdout: he was simply waited for the Japanese army to retake Lubang, and until then he had to stay alive and keep up the fight, which he did, in his way, for nearly three decades. He was confronted with leaflets and the shouted pleas of former Japanese soldiers telling him the war was over, all of which Onoda steadfastly refused to believe. Onoda would sometimes muse about how the war was going, but it never crossed his mind that Japan had actually lost. Defeat was unthinkable.

The legacy of the holdouts is a complicated one. It would easy to dismiss men like Yokoi, Onoda and Nakamura as fanatic soldiers, or simply deluded men. The term "fog of war" comes to mind to describe the mindset of the holdouts. They were misled — as all soldiers are — to believe in the might and right of their own cause; they were not worldly; they were lost and abandoned in a strange place, far from home; and they had survived what most of their comrades had not. The holdouts believed whatever they had to believe to stay alive, to keep from despair and to stay true to their sense of self.

Captain Sakae Oba

Captain Sakae Oba arrived in the South Pacific a survivor, and he left Saipan a survivor. He took part in one of the most gruesome battles of the Pacific War, the American assault on Saipan. Of the tens of thousands of Japanese, soldiers and civilians, Oba was one of the few who returned to tell his story. Captain Sakae Oba saved his small platoon from the bloodiest banzai attack in the war. He evaded capture and led attacks deep behind enemy lines, and chose to continue fighting rather than die futilely or take his own life. Against all odds he and his soldiers defended a group of two hundred Japanese civilians, many of them women, children, and elderly. He fought the Americans, narrowly escaping capture countless times, for 512 days. He and his 46 men surrendered in a formal ceremony on December 1, 1945, three months after Japan officially capitulated. Before he left Saipan, Captain Sakae Oba was feted by the same American Marine officers who had pursued him furiously across the island with no success, and who had dubbed him "the Fox."

Sakae Oba was born March 21, 1914, in the coastal town of Gamagori by Mikawa Bay. The year of his birth coincided with the Japanese occupation of the Mariana Islands in the South Pacific. Germany had purchased the Marianas from Spain in 1898 after the Spanish-American War, except for Guam, the southernmost island in the Mariana archipelago, which America took alongside Cuba, Puerto Rico, and the Philippines. In 1914, the Japanese military occupied the northern Marianas, including Saipan, and the government encouraged Japanese to settle there as agriculturalists. By the time Captain Sake Oba arrived on Saipan, there were over 20,000, more than outnumbering the native Chammorro population.

Before joining the military, Sakae Oba married his sweetheart, Mineko Hirano. In 1934, at the age of twenty, Sakae Oba enlisted in the 18th Infantry Regiment of the Imperial Japanese Army garrisoned in Gamagori. He was made an officer candidate and, after special training, was sent to join the rest of the 18th Regiment in Manchuria on occupation duty. Sakae Oba participated in the amphibious assault on Shanghai at the start of the Sino-Japanese War in 1937 before rotating back to Manchuria. For the next seven years he saw little combat but steady promotion, earning the rank of captain.

In 1944, in response to the encroaching American threat, Japanese high command moved the 18th Regiment from Manchuria to the South Pacific. On February 23, 1944, after a three-day journey south by train, Captain Sakae Oba reached Pusan, Korea. There he and 4,000 other men of the 18th Regiment traded in their winter clothes and learned their destination: Saipan. They were to be part of a convoy sending reinforcements to Japanese garrisons all over the Pacific. The men, mostly medics, tankers, and engineers, boarded the Sakuhato-Maru, a cramped, dank transport ship, and settled in for the two-week voyage to Saipan.

Most of them never made it. A week into trip, the convoy was attacked by an American submarine and the Sakuhato-Maru was sunk. Of the 4,000 men of the 18th Regiment, only 1,720 survived and were rescued. Captain Sakae Oba, injured and barely conscious, arrived on Saipan in early March. After two weeks of rest and recuperation in a field hospital, Oba was sent to work building defensive fortifications in the hills overlooking the Japanese settlement of Garapan. The lack of building materials and adequate supplies stifled his efforts. Tractors, cement, and steel were impossible to acquire. Stationed in Manchuria, Oba had heard nothing of American victories in the South Pacific, but now he saw firsthand the vulnerability of the Japanese position. Captain Oba's superiors were convinced the American attack could come any day.

On June 15, it did. One of the largest amphibious landings in history put tens of thousands of American infantrymen on beaches west and south, cutting off the two settlements of Garapan and Charan Kanoa, the homes of 25,000 Japanese and 3,000 Chamorro civilians, respectively. The landing was preceded by three days of constant bombardment from an armada of destroyers and aircraft carriers. The onslaught destroyed many Japanese emplacements, but the island was still defended by nearly 30,000 soldiers.

Captain Sakae Oba and survivors of his regiment established a medical camp away from the line of American advance. Enduring endless shelling that slowly eroded their numbers, Oba and his men treated the stream of wounded soldiers brought in from the front. The thatched-roof treatment room was soon bombed, and so they treated casualties in nearby caves, always under threat of mortar fire. After two weeks, Colonel Suzuki, the second-in-command of the Japanese forces on Saipan, activated the 18th Regiment as infantry and ordered them to attack the enemy's lines. Having watched so many of his friends die at their hands, Captain Oba relished the chance to finally strike back at the Americans.

As they marched southward along the edge of Mount Tapotchau, they passed civilians fleeing the combat. Women carrying infants, crying children, and the debris of war were all the men saw as they proceeded south to their rendezvous. They never got there. Almost demolished by mortar fire, navigating perilous ridges and canyons that skirt the 1500-foot Mount Taptchau, they were driven back to their aid station. The attempted counterattack by the scattered forces had failed, and Captain Oba received orders to abandon the camp and head for Matansha to prepare for an all-out assault. There he made the most difficult of his decisions in the war: he ordered all the men who could walk to join the march to Matansha; the rest were to be assisted to take their own lives in a manner of their choosing.

He had lost countless men to the Americans and yet he had never even seen one, let alone killed one of them. He had been forced to order the deaths of his own men. He had failed. Captain Sakae Oba knelt down and prepared to take his own life in the traditional manner of a Japanese warrior. As he knelt, dagger in hand, his second, the man who would shoot him in the head after Oba had impaled himself, told him that his death was for the good of Japan and the Imperial Army. In that moment Sakae Oba realized the futility of suicide, and that if every soldier in the Imperial Army followed his example, there would be no Imperial Army left. He rose, sheathed his blade, and resolved to die fighting instead. He composed himself, and rejoined his men on the march to Matansha.

The remaining Japanese forces, led by the aging Lt. General Saito, were boxed in the northern half of Saipan. No choices remained but whether to die by attrition or in a final counterassault. Lt. Gen. Saito's headquarters were based in the so-called "Valley of Hell," just one kilometer south of Captain Oba's abandoned medical aid station. From there he issued the order for a gyokusai, or suicidal attack, on the American lines to the south. "In death there is life," Saito told his men. Meanwhile, Vice Admiral Nagumo, the commander of the Japanese naval forces assigned to Saipan, issued a contradictory order instructing the survivors to keep fighting and to "avoid participation in an obvious suicide attack." Reinforcements were coming, but a banzai charge would leave them with nothing to reinforce.

Captain Sakae Oba and his band of soldiers rendezvoused with hundreds of other survivors at Matansha. There they learned of both Saito and Nagumo's very different orders, and each man was left to decide his own course of action. Oba elected to fight on, using Mount Tapotchau, which had a bird's-eye view of the entire island, as his base of operations. Most of the men gathered at Matansha elected to join the gyokusai.

Saito's gyokusai took place in the early hours of July 7. The night before, Saito and four other commanding officers committed suicide. The 4,000 surviving Japanese soldiers, some armed with nothing more than bayonets fixed to bamboo spears, charged the American lines west of Matansha. Flares fired from American ships offshore lit the path of their advance, mortars tore them to pieces, and machine gun fire cut them down by the dozens. It was the largest banzai charge of the Pacific War. Captain Sakae Oba led his remaining troops south and away from the carnage.

On July 9, the Admiral Turner, the American naval commander in charge of the invasion, declared Saipan officially secured. Except Oba and his men were still out there, surviving off caches of food, ammunition, and weapons scattered across the island for just such an event. They continued to harass the enemy, retreating to the rugged terrain of Mount Tapotchau when American patrols came out in search of them.

Soon they were joined by a group of a hundred and twenty-four civilians, including fifty women and children. They were the survivors: in response to twin appeals from Lt. Gen. Saito and Emperor Hirohito, thousands of Japanese civilians on Saipan had committed suicide to avoid capture. Captain Oba was now personally responsible for a group of nearly three hundred soldiers and civilians. By mid-October three camps had been established under Oba's overall command. He spent at least one day in each camp every week, checking security and addressing food and personnel issues. They built shacks out of debris, and cleared jungle for growing crops, making every effort to keep themselves concealed from American patrols. Despite their precarious position, guarding civilians surrounded by the enemy, some of the soldiers still wanted to fight. Oba retorted their primary concern was stay undetected and to survive. Oba's skill at dodging enemy patrols soon became legendary among the American Marines, who dubbed him the "Fox."

In September 1944, four months after they had declared Saipan "secured," Marine commanders began planning a massive, dragnet search operation to flush Captain Sakae Oba and his band out of the interior, where they would have to surrender, or fight. The plan was for a line of Marines, six feet apart, to march across the island, making any escape impossible. Some of the elderly and infirm volunteered to surrender to preserve the group. As Marines ransacked their huts and small gardens, the holdouts hid in a concealed clearing on a ledge above them. Apart from those who voluntarily surrendered, none of Oba's group were captured that day. The Marine commander who planned the dragnet was humiliated, and the failure of the search led to his reassignment.

The holdouts returned to their encampments, repaired the damage, and resowed their crops. They survived for another year before surrendering. Only in late November 1945, three months after the end of the war and nearly three years after the end of the Battle of Saipan, did the group finally surrender. Captain Sakae Oba was unlike many other Japanese holdouts of World War II. He did not obstinately persist out of disbelief that Japan had lost; he was not a fanatic with a "fight until the end" mentality. He and his band of followers held out in the belief that the war was ongoing, that they were cut off from their command and had to do everything they could to stay alive until communication was reestablished and new orders were given. Captain Sakae Oba had responsibilities that transcended his duties as a soldier: hundreds of Japanese civilians depended on him for leadership, guidance and protection. It was this responsibility to the defenseless that sustained him, and prevented him from despairing and throwing his life away in a "final attack," as other holdouts did after months and oftentimes years of waiting wore down their resolve.

Major General Umahachi Amo, a former commander of Japanese forces on Saipan, walked the island singing the Japanese army anthem. He managed to draw out a few of Oba's group, and told them the war was over. Amo was taken to Oba, and gave him documents from the then-defunct Imperial Army ordering the captain and his group to surrender to the Americans. On December 1, 1945, Captain Sakae Oba and his men assembled on Mt. Tapochau to sing a song of remembrance for the war-dead. Of the 30,000 Japanese soldiers and civilians on Saipan, only about a 1,000 survived: of these, close to 300 were a part of Oba's group. Captain Oba then led his people down from the mountain, where they formally surrendered their arms and colors to the Marine commander. Before being repatriated to Japan, Captain Oba was feted at the Marine Officers' Club on Saipan, where his former adversaries honored him for his skill, courage, and tenacity.

When he returned home to Japan in 1946, Captain Sakae Oba received letters from aggrieved nationalists who thought he should have died, either by dying in a banzai charge with his original unit or by committing suicide. Many surviving veterans faced the same kind of harassment upon their return from nationalists who blamed them for losing the war. These nationalist voices called upon old samurai traditions and notions of honor to justify their belief that Oba and other holdouts *should* have committed suicide in atonement for their supposed failure. Much has been said about Japanese kamikaze pilots, banzai charges, and officers who committed seppuku during and after World War II. Western cultural commentary about Japanese martial values has sometimes universalized the warrior code of the samurai, *bushido*. While the war did see a revival of certain elements of bushido, such as its precept of "death before dishonor," it would be a grievous error to impute these values to all Japanese, or to consider them as essential to Japanese culture. The Meiji Restoration of 1868 overthrew the corrupt and widely despised samurai class and discarded their value system as backwards and unsuited to the modern world. The newly formed Japanese army and navy did not initially import samurai-class morals and values: they were modeled after Western militaries, and their indoctrination did not include any orders for soldiers to commit suicide if they were captured or defeated. For its first forty years, the Japanese army was much like any other modern military. It was only after Japan had won the Sino-Japanese war of 1894-5 and the Russo-Japanese War of 1904-5 that pre-Meiji samurai codes officially entered Japanese military doctrine and indoctrination. Its victories against China and Russia had given the Japanese military an aura of invincibility. It was only in 1908 that the military revised its codes of conduct to make withdrawing, surrendering, or letting oneself be captured a criminal act. It was only by 1932, as Japanese society was becoming increasingly militarized, that being captured was considered a disgrace worthy of suicide. Only from then on were Japanese soldiers taught to prefer death to defeat.

Sources:

Don Jones. Oba: The Last Samurai, Saipan 1944-45 (Novato: Presidio, 1986).

Beatrice Trefalt, Japanese Army Stragglers and Memories of the War in Japan, 1950-75 (Routledge: London, 2003).

"Sakae Oba," accessed April 25, 2014, http://en.wikipedia.org/wiki/Sakae_Oba.

"Battle of Saipan," accessed April 26, 2014, http://en.wikipedia.org/wiki/Battle_of_Saipan.

Colonel Tsuji Masanobu

Colonel Tsuji Masanobu was a senior military tactician, an alleged war criminal, and a politician. His reputation as one of the Emperor's most fanatical servants during the Great Pacific War stands to this day. After Japan surrendered in August 1945, Colonel Tsuji and seven of his comrades went into hiding to avoid prosecution for war crimes. Tsuji returned to Japan incognito in 1947, where he lived quietly under an assumed name. He emerged in 1950, when the US removed him from the list of wanted war criminals. Tsuji wrote a number of bestselling books about his experiences in wartime and while underground, which made him something of a celebrity in Japan. He won election to the Japanese Diet in 1952, representing his native Ishikawa Prefecture. In 1961, just a week before his son graduated university, Tsuji left for Laos, engulfed in a civil war at that time. He disappeared in Laos, presumably a casualty of the war. He was declared legally dead in 1968.

Tsuji Masanobu was born in Ishikawa Prefecture in 1901, the eldest son of the respected, though dwindling, Tsuji clan. Masanobu committed himself to military service early in life. At 16, Masanobu entered the military preparatory academy at Nagoya, meant to prepare officer candidates for the Imperial Japanese Army. There he distinguished himself, and soon transferred to the military academy in Tokyo. At the age of 20, Masanobu was attached to the Army General Staff Office. He graduated from the Army War College in 1924. Masanobu's classmates from his years of military training would become his most loyal allies, during and after the Great Pacific War that would define them all.

His reputation as a brilliant student and passionate soldier firmly entrenched, Tsuji Masanobu, now a lieutenant, attended classes at the War College, disputing with his professors on matters of tactics, firmly asserting his untested theories of strategy. Masanobu was bullheaded, figuratively and literally; a diminutive man of immense personal energy with a meticulously shaved head who stared his opponents down through thick spectacles.

It was during this time that Masanobu choose his affiliation in the deeply politicized culture of the Japanese military. The more prominent faction argued for a strong military that did not meddle with politics--the Tosei faction. The narrow and radical path was represented by the Kodo, or "Imperial Way," faction, which sought to restore the Emperor to preeminence in politics with the army as his support. The Kodo faction was condemned by the top generals and the Emperor himself. In November 1934, Masanobu, now a captain and a company commander at the Tokyo military academy, learned of planned coup attempt by five cadets who were followers of the Kodo faction. Although he reported the cadets and they were expelled, Masanobu himself would repeatedly demonstrate his belief in the doctrine of "loyal insubordination," or disobeying orders or taking unilateral action when in the best interests of the Emperor.

In 1937, Tsuji Masanobu was sent to Manchuria as a staff officer of the Kwantung Army, which was occupying the region and extending the Japanese Co-Prosperity Sphere southward into China. He tried to stamp out the rampant corruption that plagued the occupying army, to no avail. The Kwantung Army was a bastion of support for the Imperial Way faction; Masanobu might even have been sent there as a spy. Regardless, he was as cantankerous and bullheaded as he had been as a student and an instructor; now, however, he was a leader of men in battle, and his stubbornness would have real consequences.

Tsuji Masanobu was the lead strategist of the so-called 1939 "Nomonhan Incident," in which the Japanese Sixth Army was decisively defeated by Russian and Mongolian forces. He ordered Japanese Sixth Army officers who had been captured to commit suicide to atone for their failure, which helped to establish in practice the Army's policy of favoring suicide over capture or defeat. The Army had revised its codes of conduct in 1908, following successive victories over China and Russia in 1895 and 1905, respectively, to make withdrawing, surrendering or allowing oneself to be captured by the enemy a criminal act. The revisions of 1908 established an ideal of invincibility that Japanese soldiers were intended to strive for, and invoked the old samurai bushido ethic. However, reinstating the practice of seppuku, or ritual suicide, took several more decades. Although the aforementioned revision of the military codes occurred in 1908, it was not until the early 1930s that being captured was considered a disgrace worthy of suicide. Officers like Colonel Tsuji Masanobu were instrumental in reestablishing suicide as an atonement for Japanese soldiers who had failed in their duty, surrendered or had been captured by the enemy.

Soon after the "Nomohan Incident," Masanobu was transferred to the South Pacific to serve as a staff officer under the "Tiger," General Yamashita, where he participated in the planning of the successful invasions of Malaya, Singapore, and Bataan. The operations had captured tens of thousands of British, Malay, Filipino, and American soldiers. Colonel Tsuji Masanobu asked the policy of Sook Ching, or ethnic cleansing, be extended to all Malaya, which led to the massacre of thousands of Chinese civilians in rural Malaya and Singapore.

After two attempts had failed to capture Guadalcanal earlier in 1942, Masanobu convinced General Yamashita to give him control over the operation. There he led a 4,600-man regiment to almost utter annihilation. A last-minute squabble with a fellow commander ruined the timing of the operation and 3,000 men were killed needlessly. He confessed this in a message to the Army Chief of Staff reporting the catastrophe which read: "They failed because I underestimated the enemy's fighting power and insisted on my own operations plans which was erroneous." After such a grave failure of judgment that cost the lives of thousands of Japanese infantrymen, Masanobu would have been justified in committing suicide by his own logic of "death before disgrace." Obviously, however, he did not apply the rule of "death before disgrace" to himself. Colonel Tsuji Masanobu reserved ritual suicide as a punishment for lower-ranking officers who had failed. If he had taken the bushido code seriously, Masanobu would have killed himself honorably long before his disastrous campaign on Guadalcanal.

Back in Tokyo after escaping Guadalcanal, Colonel Tsuji presented an appeal to the Emperor to abandon the campaign for the island, to retreat. The senior generals agreed it was the only sensible option, and Colonel Tsuji was chosen to deliver the news. The Emperor approved the evacuation, and between February 1-4, 1945, 12,000 stranded Japanese soldiers were transported off the island. Colonel Tsuji Masanobu was then transferred to Nanjing, China, presumably as punishment for being the bearer of bad news.

Soon afterwards, his spirit unbroken despite numerous setbacks, Masanobu was sent to Burma to serve in the general staff of the 33rd Army. Colonel Tsuji's reputation preceded him: the garrison in Burma was dissipated and the new colonel set about to shake it up. He gave a rousing speech to the enlisted men in the mess hall, boasting that he had the bullets of five countries in his body and the favor of the Emperor. He held a banquet for his fellow staff officers: on the menu was the skewered liver of a captured British pilot. He told them every bite they took would strengthen their resolve against the enemy; most of those present declined. Many Japanese officers who served under Tsuji made the same characterization, both during and after the war. They blamed Japan's defeat on reckless and fanatical men like Tsuji Masanobu, who had achieved power and influence in the military without attaining circumspection and foresight. Lt. General Sosaku Suzuki, who served with Tsuji on General Yamashita's staff in Malaya, compared men like the colonel to "poisonous insects" that had to be exterminated for the health of the Japanese army. While in Malaya, Colonel Tsuji unilaterally ordered the massacre of thousands of Chinese merchants—allegedly for the crime of supporting the British occupation—an act of insubordination which prompted Suzuki to request that General Yamashita punish and dismiss the out-of-control colonel. Yamashita apparently turned a blind eye to Colonel Tsuji's war crimes, hesitant to dismiss a well-connected officer even as Japan's position in Malaya quickly eroded.

Although he had campaigned in nearly every theater of the Great Pacific War, and sustained injuries in most, it was in Burma that Masanobu's luck finally ran out. The Allies captured Rangoon in December 1944, and extensive air raids cut off communications and supply lines between Japanese forces stationed in the north and south of the country.

According to the account he wrote later, Colonel Tsuji Masanobu was officially transferred to Bangkok in June 1945. More likely is that Masanobu fled the British invasion without orders, rather than take his own life, as he had demanded of his subordinates in Manchuria. On August 17th, 1945, Colonel Masanobu removed his uniform and donned the cloak of a Buddhist monk. Crossing into Vietnam, he offered his services to the Chinese Nationalist Army of Chiang Kai-shek. Masanobu was one of hundreds of Japanese servicemen who refused to surrender and instead became mercenaries for colonial and anti-colonial armies after the end of World War II. In his travels through Southeast Asia he encountered Japanese soldiers working for the Vietnamese and Chinese communists, and others like himself working for the Chinese Nationalists. He wrote manuals on cold-weather operations, basic training, and the likelihood of World War III. He spent six months translating a 1924 Japanese army manual about fighting Russia in Siberia. Masanobu tried to make himself appear useful to his employers; after all, his fate was far better than many of his comrades. Writing reports, translating manuals, appearing useful, he learned that Japanese were being held in POW camps in Manchuria, the site of his first assignment. It was essentially busywork to convince the Nationalists he was of use to them, to avoid being sent to a POW camp. Masanobu, as an intelligence asset, was relatively well treated, although he was not free to leave. The conditions of his work still galled him though; he called his attachment, the Third Research Group, a "miserable intelligence unit." His stubbornness and prepossession had survived the war intact. Masanobu was in no position to complain: in Nanjing, his former classmates and comrades-in-arms were on trial for war crimes.

He spent most of late 1947 and early 1948 translating a captured, multi-volume Japanese army report on the Soviet military--the Chinese, Nationalist and Communist, were as hungry as the Americans for intelligence on the Soviets. Colonel Tsuji Masanobu was one of thousands of war criminals who escaped prosecution by offering their services to the victors. By February 1948 he had completed the translation and sanctimoniously submitted his resignation to the Nationalist army. Most of the Japanese on the mainland-- apart from technicians, specialists, and war criminals, of course--had been repatriated by mid-1948. Using an assumed name, Masanobu boarded a ship bound for Japan on May 16. On the same vessel were several military men Masanobu knew personally, being repatriated to stand trial in Japan; the men did not recognize their former comrade.

On May 26, 1948, he arrived at Sasebo, Nagasaki, kissing the ground beneath his feet. For the next two years he lived under an assumed name, claiming various cover stories, acquiring a penchant for mysterious behavior he would maintain until his disappearance in 1961. On New Year's Day, 1950, the Allied War Tribunals concluded, and Tsuji Masanobu was officially removed from the list of wanted war criminals. He was a free man.

Apparently, Masanobu had been writing while he was underground, because he soon published an autobiography of his years in hiding--he excluded his wartime exploits--which became an instant bestseller in post-war Japan. Colonel Tsuji Masanobu became a national celebrity. In public at least, no one called him a coward for going into hiding; no one suggested he should have committed suicide after his many failures. Masanobu narrowly escaped the fates of war criminals and "holdouts": to be executed or to be called a coward. Instead, he attained to high office. He ran for a seat in the House of Representatives in 1952, easily winning in his native Ishikawa Prefecture.

In fact, Colonel Tsuji Masanobu was still in demand even as an intelligence officer. Recently declassified documents reveal the CIA attempted to recruit Masanobu after he came out of hiding. The CIA evaluation said what Masanobu's superiors never did, whether because of his personal charisma, self-assurance, or his rumored connections with the Imperial family: "In either politics or intelligence work, he is hopelessly lost both by reason of personality and lack of experience... Tsuji is the type of man who, given the chance, would start World War III without any misgivings." Many Japanese Army officers considered men like Colonel Tsuji Masanobu the very reason for Japan's defeat: they blamed him for being unwilling to face reality, unwilling to admit fault and change strategy, and they were right. Everywhere he went, Colonel Tsuji needlessly spent the lives of his subordinated and eroded the morale of those who survived his reckless command.

And, indeed, his political career was marked by the same erratic behavior that characterized his military service. He continued in politics the practice of gekokujo, or "loyal insubordination," which he acquired as an officer, and led to numerous war crimes, such as the massacre of Chinese civilians in Malaya and Singapore. The year after he was elected, Tsuji Masanobu founded a society that denounced the American presence in Japan and advocated for immediate military rearmament to prepare for a second war against the United States. The CIA assessment of Masanobu as "hopelessly lost" seems especially accurate in this context.

Tsuji Masanobu wrote several additional bestsellers while in office, including a boastful account of his role in planning the 1942 capture of Singapore, titled "Japan's Greatest Victory, Britain's Worst Defeat," which helped him win election to the Diet's House of Councilors in 1959. The book deals only with the planning and the battle; not with the massacres of Chinese civilians that came after. He appealed to the militarist right-wing elements in Japan who were bitter about losing the war. He was expelled from the Liberal Democratic Party in 1959 for insubordination and criticizing the Prime Minister, who was himself an alleged war criminal.

In 1961, he left for Laos, embroiled in a vicious civil war at the time, telling his wife and son that he had been given a "special mission" by the Prime Minister; this was probably fanciful, but served to avoid arousing suspicion. Why he left, and what became of him, remains a mystery. He sent his last postcard to his younger brother on April 20, 1961: "I saw Laos," it read, "War and festivals are taking place at the same time and in the same place."

Sources:

Shiro Yoneyama, "Disappearance of Tsuji Masanobu remains a mystery," The Japan Times, July 26, 2000.

"The Pacific War Online Encyclopedia: Tsuji Masanobu," Pacific War Online Encyclopedia, accessed May 1, 2014, http://pwencycl.kgbudge.com/T/s/Tsuji_Masanobu.htm.

"Colonel Tsuji Masanobu," accessed May 2, 2014, http://www.warbirdforum.com/tsuji.htm.

Lt. Ei Yamaguchi

Lt. Ei Yamaguchi was one of the only survivors of the vicious Battle of Peleliu. The Americans invaded the tiny South Pacific island in September 1944 and captured it from the 10,000 Japanese defenders after two months of fierce, stalemated combat. After the battle was over, Lt. Ei Yamaguchi shepherded 33 other survivors for two years from a base high up in Peleliu's Umurbogol ridge. They harassed the small Marine detachment left behind to guard Peleliu, and dreamed of taking back the island. Yamaguchi and his 33 holdouts survived on rations pilfered from the Marines, and occasionally harassed them with rifle fire and grenade attacks, but their primary concern was to survive. In April 1947, nearly two years after the end of the war, Lt. Ei Yamaguchi and his band surrendered to the Marines.

The Battle of Peleliu was one of the most bitterly fought battles in the Pacific Theatre of World War II. Peleliu, an island in the present-day country of Palau, is equidistant to the Philippines and New Guinea, which put it high on the list of targets during the American island-hopping campaign in the South Pacific. Preparations on the Japanese side were intense. Japanese high command knew that Peleliu was a strategic defensive point and they were determined, after setbacks in Saipan and Guam, not to let it go without a fight.

When the 2nd Infantry Regiment, which included 2nd Lt. Ei Yamaguchi and his soon-to-be band of 33 holdouts, landed on Peleliu, they were "astonished at the weakness of the island." They were immediately set to work at building new ramparts and defensive fortifications and revamping existing ones. (LMS, p. 31) They worked with their hands, with shovels and improvised implements; they worked with bamboo, with rock, sand and driftwood, whatever was on hand. Geography and nature were set against them: the beach was a thin stretch without much in the way of natural defensive positions. They used what rock outcroppings, ridgelines and sand dunes presented themselves to them: lacking concrete and steel, bolstering natural defensive positions was their only choice. Although it seemed desperate to them at the time, it turned out to be a decent strategy: using natural cover and dug-out caves and rock outcroppings effectively camouflaged the Japanese positions, and landing American Marines often moved unwittingly straight into the Japanese line-of-fire, not recognizing a pillbox as a pillbox.

Colonel Tada of the 2nd Infantry Regiment, another survivor of the Battle of Peleliu, held no illusions. "'We did not believe this method of attack would succeed.'" (LMS, p. 31) The 2nd Infantry Regiment was thoroughly alone on Peleliu. They had no air support of any kind. They had no armored vehicles capable of defeating American tanks. The strategy was not to achieve victory in a decisive battle--the overly direct approach that lost the Japanese so many of their island holdings in the Pacific--but to make the cost of holding Peleliu so high the Americans would withdraw. Unfortunately, as Colonel Tada well knew, the best time to impose the highest cost on the enemy was during their landing. Every American they killed on the beach was one less American they had to kill in the jungle. Effective defensive structures, interlocking fields-of-fire, anti-personnel and anti-tank emplacements were indispensable to this strategy, and they were exactly what the Japanese lacked on Peleliu. The Japanese infantrymen would have to make do with bamboo ramparts, basic weapons and simple dug-out foxholes and defensive embankments. They did not have the equipment—such as tractors, the lack of which destroyed countless Japanese positions in the South Pacific—to build a defensive line that would impose a high cost on the Americans as they were landing. They would do what they had to, they would do their best to give the Americans a hellish welcome on Peleliu, and then abandon the line and draw the Americans into the jungle and, hopefully, into a protracted and exhausting campaign that would persuade them to leave the island. It was a desperate strategy; however, it was the only one available to the Japanese.

Colonel Nakagawa, the commander of the Japanese forces and Lt. Ei Yamaguchi's ultimate superior on the island, divided the tiny island into four defensive sectors. He assigned the crucial western sector to the 2nd Infantry Regiment, Lt. Ei Yamaguchi's outfit. Colonel Nakagawa's second-in-command, Captain Sakamoto, was put in control of the western sector. The one thousand men of the 2nd Battalion, 2nd Infantry Regiment, were expected to bare the brunt of the Allied landing without artillery or tank support. Lt. Ei Yamaguchi's job, although they may have known it at the time, was merely to slow the advance of the Allied landing, which his superiors thought inevitable. The beach on the western coast of Peleliu was razor-thin: the 2nd Infantry would have nowhere to retreat to when the Allies landed on 15 September 1944. The 2nd Infantry Regiment set up mortar and machine-gun positions with interlocking fields of fire along the beach. In the event the Americans established a firm beachhead, their orders from Colonel Nakagawa were to "attack and destroy them that night at the latest," and to "maintain a firm hold on the high ground." If the enemy seized the beach, remaining forces were to launch "daring guerrilla warfare" against them from the easily defensible high ground. Little did Lt. Yamaguchi or the other men of the 2nd Infantry Regiment know their superiors considered their task, to hold the beachhead, nearly hopeless. Colonel Nakagawa was merely implementing the lessons learned from the Japanese defeats at Saipan and Guam: the strategy was not to hold the Americans at the beach, but to inflict maximum casualties while conducting a staged retreat. (LMS, p. 33)

By the time the Allied invasion hit Peleliu, the Japanese had changed their tactics significantly. The old method of trying to hold the enemy at the beach had failed repeatedly: it was abandoned. Banzai attacks were repudiated by Japanese high command as wasteful and ineffective. The Japanese high command tried to communicate the new tactics as much as possible to the infantrymen on the ground; although change was not something that came easily to the Japanese military. There was also an institutional squabble to deal with. Army generals insisted pridefully that their men could hold the beach no matter the cost, while Navy admirals—who were the most pragmatic force in the Japanese armed forces—would insist on guerrilla tactics to prolong the conflict. It was a matter of pride and pragmatism colliding with reality. However much the official tactics of the Japanese military had changed as a result of the success of the Allies' island-hopping campaign, many junior officers still considered not holding the beach a failure and ordered useless suicide attacks to make up for it. In some cases, ground officers received entirely contradictory orders from the two branches: the Army generals told them to hold the beach, while Navy admirals radioed that they should head for the hills and employ guerrilla tactics.

The Americans landed in the early morning of September 15, 1944. The Japanese preparations paid off: Lt. Yamaguchi and the men of the 2nd Infantry Regiment inflicted heavy casualties on the Americans at the beach. They followed orders, inflicting casualties as they withdrew to higher ground. Their strategic retreat left them at the highest, most easily defended point of Peleliu: the so-called "Bloody Nose" ridge that ran parallel to the island's length.

After these setbacks, the Japanese resorted to fukakku, or "endurance engagements" meant to prolong the conflicts. Even before the Allies landed, Colonel Nakagawa and other Japanese commanders, mindful of the fate of some many other islands that had fallen, tried to avoid large, fixed engagements and suicidal "banzai" attacks. As Major Raymond Davis described it, "'The Japs were in deep caves, which had small holes for fixed machine gun fire. We were being hit from all sides with no way to get at them.'" (LMS, p. 31)

The beach fell decisively within a week, with heavy casualties for both the Americans and the Japanese; the fighting along the "Bloody Nose" ridge would last over two months, with "every foxhole and cave position ... defended to the death." The Americans used napalm to burn out the defensive positions, almost entirely incinerating the "Bloody Nose" ridge. Lt. Yamaguchi and his band of 33 holdouts were among the last of only a few hundred Japanese soldiers to survive the months-long battle.

As the sun was setting on November 24, Colonel Nakagawa burned his uniform and committed ritual suicide in atonement for losing the island. He was posthumously promoted to the rank of lieutenant general. On November 27, Major Raymond Davis declared Peleliu secured. The scale of the Japanese defeat must have shocked Lt. Ei Yamaguchi: of the 11,000 Japanese defenders, nearly all were killed. Only 300 men survived the months-long battle. Most of the survivors were captured, surrendered, committed suicide, or were killed. Soon the American force was reduced to a mere caretaker regiment of 150 Marines to guard the island. Although the Marines knew there were still a few Japanese, apart from an occasional patrol they did little to hunt them.

Lt. Ei Yamaguchi was not trained in guerrilla warfare. His tactics were inspired by the exigencies of war and the last orders of his superior officers. The idea of fighting a "one-man war" like Lt. Hiro Onoda on Lubang Island never would never have occurred to Lt. Ei Yamaguchi. The training that Lt. Yamaguchi received was that of any infantry officer. He had not studied guerrilla warfare tactics at the Nakano School, like Hiro Onoda had, or been trained by Nakano graduates, like Teruo Nakamura. His primary concern was to maintain the cohesiveness of his remaining troopers; he never would have considered abandoning them in order to be more effective, as Lt. Onoda and Private Nakamura did.

The greatest challenge Lt. Ei Yamaguchi faced, apart from dodging American patrols and the occasional mortar strike, was simply to keep his unit cohesive. Many holdouts found collaborating with others the hardest part of survival. Some among his band wanted to surrender, to be sure, and it is a testament to Lt. Ei Yamaguchi's skill as a commander that he kept them fighting for two and a half years without contact or support from their headquarters. It is likely that many of his band were recent recruits, or had not seen much combat previous to Peleliu, and believed the army propaganda promising a "decisive victory" any day. Lt. Yamaguchi was able to convince himself and dozens of others that the war was ongoing, that they still had a duty to uphold. As he said decades later, "We couldn't believe we had lost. We were always instructed that we could never lose. It is the Japanese tradition that we must fight until we die, until the end." (NBC Dateline, 1995) Ultimately, however, it was the desertion of one of Lt. Yamaguchi's subordinates, Superior Seaman Tsuchida, that precipitated the band's surrender in late April 1947. They survived by pilfering supplies from the American detachment left behind to guard the island. The Marines would occasionally send out patrols. They never found Lt. Yamaguchi and his 33, high in the Umurbrogol, a treacherous ridge carved out by volcanic activity that traverses Peleliu. They hid in an intricate network of caves, some left over from the battle, some natural, the rest dug out with scavenged tools. As the months turned into years, the vegetation which had been destroyed by mortars and napalm slowly grew back; the burnt, desolated landscape of the war grew lush, verdant, and peaceful again. All they could do, Lt. Ei Yamaguchi and his band of 33 holdouts, was harass the Allies' rear, compel them to send in reinforcements, to divert their wrath from the Home Islands. They rarely managed more than potshots at the remaining Marines, however; ammo was scarce, and their primary concerns were survival and staying undetected.

Yamaguchi was partially motivated by a sense of duty, and partly by a simple unwillingness to believe the war was over. He arrived on Peleliu fresh from training, and in his perspective, cloistered by army and government propaganda, the war was only beginning. Although the Japanese defended Peleliu for two solid months, and made it one of the bitterest battles the Americans fought in the Pacific, Lt. Yamaguchi felt he had been robbed of the opportunity to prove himself. He hadn't fought long enough, hadn't inflicted enough damage on the enemy; the war couldn't be over so soon. However, it might be said that Lt. Yamaguchi was also simply continuing the tactics the 2nd Infantry Regiment had used since the start of the Allied invasion of Peleliu. His aim was to make the cost of holding Peleliu higher than its strategic value, to force the Allies either to withdraw or send in reinforcements, thus weakening their attacks elsewhere in the Pacific.

For 2nd Lt. Ei Yamaguchi, the overarching failure of his commanders, the leaders of his country, became for a short time his own personal failure. His failure to hold the beach, as so many other Japanese soldiers had died trying to do on islands across the Pacific, became his burden. Guerrilla warfare had taken its toll on the Americans, to be sure; it also took its toll on the remaining Japanese. They craved for resolution, an end to the indeterminacy of unconventional, jungle warfare. They longed to face the enemy, to win or die at last. In April 1947, Lt. Yamaguchi began planning for a final banzai attack on the 150 Marines remaining on Peleliu. Most of his men, tired and demoralized, were ready for the end--but not all of them.

Senior Seaman Tsuchida, learning of the planned banzai attack, fled the holdouts' base in Umurbogol and surrendered to the American Marine detachment. The Marines went on high alert and called in reinforcements. On April 21 and 22, Seaman Tsuchida brought letters from Japan to the holdouts, telling them the war was over. In late April 1947, Lt. Ei Yamaguchi and his 33 holdouts surrendered formally to the Marines on Peleliu. The remnants of the Battle of Peleliu, rusted ships, landing vehicles, and the caves of Lt. Yamaguchi's band of holdouts, still litter the small island. In 1994, Ei Yamaguchi returned to Peleliu to commemorate the fiftieth anniversary of the battle. Yamaguchi was interviewed by NBC's Dateline in 1995: asked why he did not surrender earlier, he replied, "We couldn't believe that we had lost. We were always instructed that we could never lose. It is the Japanese tradition that we must fight until we die, until the end."

Sources:

Bill Sloan, Brotherhood of Heroes: The Marines at Peleliu --
The Bloodiest Battle of the Pacific War (New York: Simon and
Schuster, 2005).

Dick Camp, Last Man Standing: The 1st Marine Regiment on
Peleliu, September 15-21, 1944 (Minneapolis: MBI Publishing,
2010).

Susan Provost Beller, Battle in the Pacific: Soldiering in World
War II (Minneapolis: Twenty-First Century, 2008).

Lt. Hiro Onoda

Lt. Hiro Onoda was a Japanese intelligence officer, a holdout who survived the Battle of Lubang, refused to surrender to the victorious Americans, and waged a one-man thirty-year war against them, from 1945 to 1972. Although he was not the last Japanese holdout to emerge from hiding after World War II, Lt. Onoda is certainly the most well-known. Onoda refused to believe the war was over, deafening himself to the pleas of his commanders and even his family members that he surrender and come home. In 1972, a young Japanese backpacker, Norio Suzuki, went to Lubang in the hope of finding the mysterious Lt. Onoda, who had eluded capture and detection for decades. The young Suzuki finally succeeded where scores of soldiers had failed: he found Hiro Onoda, and was able to convince him the war was over.

Onoda arrived on Lubang Island on the eve of 1945. His orders were straightforward: to blow up the airfield and the pier in order to deny the enemy access the island, and to interrupt as much as possible the invasion of Luzon, Philippines. The Lubang Garrison he found were decimated, deprived, and had lost the will to fight. The garrison had more men than guns and was thoroughly unprepared for what was to come. Initially they thought Onoda had come to relieve them, to get them home, or at least to Manila, safely. Onoda explained there would be no retreat. He was there, he told the ragged men, to lead them in guerrilla warfare. The commander of the garrison had misinterpreted the message and thought that Onoda had come to take them off the island. Onoda's disgust and righteous indignation mounted as he got to know the men he had been sent to command. They had no will to fight: they were worse than useless. Onoda regretted that, as a mere second lieutenant, he had no real authority to whip the men into shape.
(NS, pg. 52)

He did not have much time to contemplate his mission: on the morning of January 3, 1945, the garrison sighted the enemy fleet--"the sea was literally peppered with landing craft" (NS, p. 54) Onoda recalled. He tried to rouse the men to the necessity of guerrilla warfare. "They all talked big about committing suicide and giving up their lives for the emperor. Deep down they were hoping and praying that Lubang would not be attacked." (NS, p. 57)

It was too late for "wishful thinking" as Onoda put it--the Battle of Luzon had begun. The strategic island of Leyte to the east of the Philippines had fallen to the Allies in December, shortly before Onoda arrived on Lubang to the west. The Allies landed on Lubang in force on February 28.

Within four days the Japanese garrision had been overrun and its remnants splintered across the 200 square mile island. Second Lieutenant Hiro Onoda was the last commissioned officer remaining in his group of twenty, and "so far as I could tell," he later wrote, "I was the only Japanese officer left on the island." Onoda had wanted a command, and suddenly he had one. The group included Corporal Shoichi Shimada and Private First Class Kinshichi Kozuka, men who would become Onoda's long-time comrades-in-arms on Lubang.

In early April Onoda ordered the group to split up into cells of three men each to avoid the ever-increasing likelihood of detection and capture. Bickering and infighting over food also contributed to the decision. Onoda rationed the rice to the cells and calculated it would last them until August. Onoda's original cell consisted of himself, Kozuka, and Shimada. He chose them for his cell because they were strong, resourceful, disciplined, and most importantly, they had not lost hope. American "clean-up squads" roamed the island, firing on any Japanese who did not immediately surrender. Onoda's cell encountered the traumatized survivors of failed banzai attacks wandering aimlessly through the jungle, many of whom were simply desperate to find food and avoid the Allies. One by one, Onoda learned of the other cells being captured or killed.

It was in the middle of October that Onoda's cell saw the first leaflet urging them to surrender. Another group of holdouts had killed a cow and were taking it back to their camp when they stumbled across five or six islanders. The islanders fled when they saw the group had guns, but they left behind a leaflet printed in Japanese. It read, "The war ended on August 15. Come down from the mountains!" Because the "clean-up squads" were still operating, however, Onoda's cell concluded the leaflet was a trick and the war was ongoing.

A second set of leaflets rained down from Boeing B-17's in December. The surviving cells gathered to consider the message. The leaflet used awkward language, had printing errors, and referenced a "Direct Imperial Order" from General Yamashita; none of the men, including a law school graduate, had ever heard of a "Direct Imperial Order," and so they suspected it of being a forgery. "There was no doubt in our minds that this was an enemy trick," Onoda affirmed. (NS, pg. 77)

What compelled this young man to ignore the pleas of his countrymen to return? To stay in the jungle rather than go home?

The explanation may partially be found in Onoda's special training. Onoda was an intelligence officer, a spy trained in propaganda and misdirection. In the leaflets urging him to surrender, Onoda saw merely the tricks of his enemy; a move in a cat-and-mouse game of deception. He had been trained to see enemy ploys in everything, and that training blinded him to the obviousness of the truth. Unlike most Japanese soldiers during the Second World War, Onoda had received intense preparation for unconventional warfare. His education in guerrilla warfare inured him to defeat. There is no such thing as defeat in unconventional warfare. Guerrillas don't go home; the battlefield is their home.

Although Onoda had trained in unconventional guerrilla warfare tactics at the Nakano School and undoubtedly made an apt pupil, he relied on his teammates as much as his training in order to survive. Onoda's comrade Kozuka, a strong young man raised on a farm, taught him many of the methods he relied on in the years to come to hunt, forage, and remain undetected. Onoda was born a survivor, trained to be a fierce guerrilla warrior, but he honed his practical skills with the help of his comrades.

As his rice supply dwindled, Onoda turned to bananas and coconuts, plentiful fruits on Lubang. His staple food for nearly thirty years was underripe bananas boiled in coconut milk. "The result tasted like overcooked sweet potatoes," Onoda reported. He did not like it, but it kept him alive. About three times a year his cell would kill a cow as stealthily as possible to dry the beef for a long-term food source. To supplement their meat supply, they built snares and traps to catch rats and other small game. They would occasionally sneak into the lowland villages to pilfer food and supplies, which sometimes brought them into direct conflict with the Lubang islanders.

Onoda and his cell would sleep outside during the dry season. Their shelters during the rainy season consisted of scaffolded lean-toes covered in coconut leaves and tied together with vines. Onoda remarked upon his return to Japan, "during my entire 30 years on Lubang, I never once slept soundly through the night." The lean-toes consisted of a bamboo pole posted against a rock or other outcropping. Their conditions were, as Onoda reminisced years later, extremely primitive. Although a graduate of the prestigious Nakano School of counterintelligence and intimately familiar with the tactics of espionage, sabotage and propaganda, Onoda and his comrades struggled to master the basics of survival in a hostile environment. Many of the techniques Onoda developed during his thirty-year guerrilla campaign have been studied by the special forces branches of countless armies. Onoda initially lit his fires by removing the gunpowder from rusty cartridges and igniting it with a lens. To conserve ammo he soon learned how to make a fire with split bamboo. As surprising as it may seem in retrospect, such basic survival skills such as making a fire using natural tools and sources of ignition was not commonly taught in the armed forces of any country at the time. Hiro Onoda's emergence after thirty years cut off from all support highlighted the need to include survival skills as part of every soldier's basic training.

During this time Onoda nursed the dream of completing his secret and solemn mission: destroying Lubang's airfield and deepwater pier as he was meant to have done at the beginning of the Battle of Luzon. When he approached the strongly guarded facility Onoda despaired of ever being able to sabotage it and, even if he could, he had no way of conveying his success up the chain of command. Survival, harassment and observation became his top priorities. In the back of his mind, however, was always his mission, the pier and the airfield. Recall that Lubang was Onoda's first assignment, and his matriculation from the Nakano School and deployment came rather late in the war. Destroying the pier and airfield on Lubang was the first and only mission Onoda received during the war, and his failure to complete it frustrated him, but it also motivated him. As long as the pier and airfield remained intact, Onoda still had a job to do, or at least to dream of doing. Maintaining such a long-term goal helped to keep Onoda focused, on-point and saved him from the despair of lacking purpose.

Onoda's position of authority held a major place in his mind, and partly explains why he refused to surrender for so long. His men relied on him, trusted him, and followed his orders, not always without question, but always with respect Onoda deserved. He was intelligent, educated, and confident. What a relief it must have been for those men to see an officer, cultivated, well-trained, indomitable, leading them through the dark, apparently quite sure of himself. And what a burden it must have been for Onoda, to see his men, hungry, demoralized, desperate, look to him for guidance and strength of will. It was only 2 years after losing his last companion, Kozuka, that Onoda finally surrendered. Having lost his subordinates, Onoda lost a large part of his motivation to continue the struggle.

The man who finally brought Onoda down from the mountain, Norio Suzuki, was young, impressionable, and thoroughly respectful. Suzuki was a young backpacker out to see the world, and meeting the mysterious Lt. Onoda was top on his list. Suzuki harkened back to Onoda's earlier days on Lubang when he had men to command, men who looked up to him, men who relied on him. Had it not been Suzuki who went looking for Onoda, the wiry old lieutenant might have died on the island. Suzuki reminded Onoda of the fresh-faced, idealistic youths he seen in training and had watched die during the Battle of Luzon. Onoda, the teacher, could only accept counsel from an idealistic young man such as Suzuki, just as he had earlier learned how to survive the jungle with the help of Kozuka and Shimada. Suzuki explained to Onoda that the war had ended years ago, that Japan was now allied with the United States, and that Onoda himself had become something of a legend, a mythical figure and a ghost of the past. What flurries of propaganda leaflets, unrelenting voices shouting over bullhorns in the wilderness and thirty years of solitude had failed to do, to persuade Lt. Onoda that the war was over and his service concluded, Norio Suzuki accomplished with just a few hours of conversation. It is fair to say that without the intervention of Norio Suzuki, Onoda would have died on Lubang, firm in his belief that he was still fighting for his country.

The standard interpretation is that Onoda refused to believe the war was over and that is why he continued fighting. This is not true. Onoda surely knew the war was over, the demoralized troops and the "wishful thinking" of their officers he encountered when he arrived at Lubang surely gave him his first indication of that. However, his guerrilla training had taught him that a war is never lost until the last soldier gives up fighting. His wild interpretations of bulletins dropped from planes were not delusional, but exactly what he needed to believe to keep himself and his men fighting. For Lt. Onoda, as long as he kept fighting, the war could still be won. He turned himself into the personal embodiment of the never-ending struggle.

For Second Lt. Onoda, the war had ended before it had even begun properly. He arrived on Lubang, fresh out of training, just two months before the Allies landed, and just eight months before the end of the war. He had expected to fight, and had prepared himself to die, but history dashed his hopes. How could he accept defeat after such a short time on the battlefield? As his comrade Shimada had often said, before he was killed by Philippine police in May 1954, "Don't worry, it'll all be back in our hands tomorrow" (NS, pg. 104). Shimada's motto must have been the spirit Onoda maintained during his thirty years on Lubang. His strength of will and faith triumphed over his environment, over the passage of time, and even over his own common sense.

When he finally surrendered in 1974, "the past seemed like a dream." Onoda confessed, "What a fool I had been!" "What had I been doing all these years?," he asked himself. (Independent, based off interview). He was honored as a hero in Japan, misguided but determined. A symbol of the resolve that Japan had summoned during the war, and the kind of men that it had created. The citizens of Lubang remembered the friends and family members that Onoda and his comrades killed over the many years.

Regardless of how Onoda felt about himself, he was welcomed in Japan as a hero, the embodiment of Japanese dedication and strength of will. He penned his memoirs, titled "My Thirty-Year War." Onoda later founded and taught classes at his own survival school; he wanted to pass on the skills he acquired on Lubang to the next generation of Japanese. He went back to Lubang in 1996, and attempted to make amends for his many acts of banditry by donating money to build a new school. Onoda remained unimpressed by post-war Japan, which traded ferocity for luxury and lost the spirit that had kept him alive on Lubang for nearly three decades. Hiro Onoda, known as the last samurai, died in Tokyo on January 16, 2014, at the age of 91.

Sources:

Hiro Onoda, No Surrender: My Thirty-year War, trans. Charles Terry (Kodansha: Tokyo, 1974).

Beatrice Trefalt, Japanese Army Stragglers and Memories of the War in Japan, 1950-75 (Routledge: London, 2003).

"Hiroo Onoda," accessed April 16, 2014,
http://en.wikipedia.org/wiki/Hiroo_Onoda.

David McNeill, "Hiroo Onoda, the last Japanese soldier to give
himself in: 'When I surrendered, the past seemed like a
dream,'" The Guardian, January 17, 2014, accessed March 5,
2014.

Private Teruo Nakamura

In 1974, Teruo Nakamura became the last "holdout" of the Imperial Japanese Army to be found after the end of the Great Pacific War in August 1945. Like Hiro Onoda, the second-to-last so-called "holdout" to emerge from hiding, Nakamura was enlisted late in the war. Unlike Onoda, however, Teruo Nakamura was not a native Japanese person. Nakamura was born in 1919 in Taiwan and was a member of Taiwan's indigenous Amis population. He was the son of native farmers, and led a rather simple life in Japanese-occupied Taiwan. His name was a legacy of Japan's policy of cultural assimilation, which tried to "Nipponize" occupied populations.

In 1943, he volunteered to join a unit of the Imperial Japanese Army. The Takasago Volunteers were a special forces unit of the IJA composed entirely of Amis men commanded by Japanese officers. The IJA thought the Amis were more aptly suited to carry out guerrilla warfare in the tropical and subtropical theatres than ethnic Japanese. The Amis came from a self-sufficient hunter-gatherer culture and possessed considerable survival skills even before training. The Takasago Volunteers were trained in unconventional warfare and intelligence gathering by officers of the Nakano School, the same school that graduated Lt. Hiro Onoda shortly before his assignment to Lubang. Lt. Onoda was in fact trained to teach and command indigenous guerrilla warriors exactly like those of the Takasago Volunteers.

Teruo Nakamura volunteered for the Takasago Volunteers in November 1943 at the age of 24. We can only speculate on his motivation; he may have seen it as a way to move up in the world. The Japanese had colonized Taiwan in 1895 and begun a process of cultural assimilation, forcing Amis people to adopt Japanese names and to speak Japanese, if possible. Teruo Nakamura was born into a period of cultural flux, caught between the modern, powerful Japanese and the ancient, subjugated Amis. Like many other conquered peoples, he may have identified more with the conquerors than with his own people. The Takasago Volunteers were highly regarded special forces and their members were accorded great esteem by their enemies and their Japanese officers. By joining their ranks, Nakamura acquired prestige and distinction, precisely what he was denied under Japanese rule as a simple indigenous farmer. The theory that he was compelled to join the Volunteers doesn't stand up: conscripts make good cannon fodder, not good special forces.

After his training at the hands of Nakano School officers, Neruo Takamura was attached to the 4th Takasago Volunteer Unit and sent to the Indonesian island of Morotai. He arrived early in 1944, just 9 months before the Allied invasion that would take the island.

Morotai is the northernmost island of the Moluccas, an island chain orientated north-south and locate in between New Guinea and Sulawesi. Morotai is a thickly forested island with an area of almost 700 square miles, and a rugged topography. If Teruo Nakamura had to choose any place to hide, Morotai was as good as any.

Before the Allied invasion began on September 15, 1944, the IJA soldiers stationed on the island numbered only 500. The Allied invaders, with 50,000 men, outnumbered the Japanese and Amis soldiers by more than one hundred to one. The IJA had attempted to deceive the Allies into believing Morotai was more heavily guarded by building fake camps and dummy airplanes; however, they were not fooled. After only a few weeks of fighting--the first combat Private Teruo Nakamura had ever seen--the Allies had effectively taken Morotai. The survivors continued to harass the Allies from hideouts in the jungle, but disease and malnutrition slowly eroded their remaining numbers.

In the first few days of 1945, after a final banzai attack had failed and radio contact between Tokyo and Morotai had been lost, the surviving Japanese commanders gave the order to the remaining troops to "enter the jungle, become self-sufficient and carry on guerrilla warfare."
(JASMW, p. 162)

From early 1945 to some time in 1946 or 1947, Private Teruo Nakamura survived in the jungles of Morotai as part of a group of survivors. They believed, or at least hoped, that the Allied capture of the island was only a temporary setback, and that the IJA would soon retake the island. Until that time, their task was to survive and to harass the Allied rear.

Sometime in 1946 or 1947, Private Teruo Nakamura left the group and struck out into the jungle to fend for himself. It is unclear why he did this; however, we can speculate based on the composition of the survivors and the experiences of other "stragglers," such as Hiro Onoda.

The survivors of the Battle of Morotai were Japanese and Amis, or indigenous Taiwanese. The Amis were targeted for recruitment into guerrilla warfare units based on their reputation of hardiness, self-sufficiency, and jungle survivability, a reputation which was well-earned. Within months of the Allied capture of Lubang, Lt. Onoda, the second-to-last holdout to emerge from hiding, ordered his group of twenty survivors to split up into cells of three to four men; the men chose their own cellmates. This served three purposes: 1) to lower the risk of detection and capture; 2) to make food-gathering a smaller task; 3) to reduce tensions between the men. Lt. Onoda wrote years later that he could not afford to burden himself with a "group of disorderly, irresponsible soldiers" (NS, p. 76). Within a year of this decision, almost all the cells had succumbed to disease or starvation, or death or capture by the Allies. Those that survived the first year were resilient and committed.

When Private Nakamura left the group in 1946-47, it may have been because of personal tensions with other soldiers, or because he thought being part of a large group increased the chance of capture; or, more likely, he had become tired of fending for other survivors who could not fend for themselves. Yoshida Jiro, an Amis volunteer who was part of a group that surrendered on Morotai in December 1955, indicated that "the Japanese soldiers who had been with [the Amis] might not have survived without them." As he put it: "It was really good for the Japanese that we were there. We were good at catching eels, and growing vegetables. When they were out of food, we helped them over and over again. But when we got back to Japan, everyone was quite unfriendly." (JASMW, p. 168).

When Private Nakamura left the group in 1946-47, it is possible that he was simply tired of holding up the dead weight of Japanese soldiers with minimal survival skills; not to mention being regarded as an inferior because he was only a private and an Amis. So he left.

In 1950, after three to four years of solitude in the jungles of Morotai, Private Teruo Nakamura joined up with Yoshida Jiro's group. However, by the time this group surrendered in December 1955, Private Teruo Nakamura had already struck out on his own once more. Exactly why he left is a debated issue. According to Nakamura, the other holdouts had threatened him and he left in fear of his life. The other holdouts denied this, saying that he left of his own accord and when he did not return they assumed he had died in the jungle. In fact, Private Nakamura had begun construction on "Nakamura City," the site that was to be his home for the next twenty years.

"Nakamura City"--as the newspapers called it when Private Teruo Nakamura was arrested in 1974--was a tiny thatched-grass hut and a 600 square-meter vegetable patch fenced off with bamboo. "Nakamura City" was perfectly situated, ensconced in a high mountain valley protected on two sides by cliffs and surrounded by dense jungle.

There Private Teruo Nakamura lived, forgotten by the world. In his garden he grew red peppers, pawpaw (papaya), taro, cassava, and other vegetables. He harvested the wild bananas and coconuts that grow plentifully on the island. He caught fish and eels in the nearby mountain rivers and streams. He still had a rifle, although he never used it to hunt. The gun would only attract attention and risk revealing his existence. (JASMW, p. 161, 163) He lived quietly. He apparently never disturbed the natives of Morotai, who numbered over 10,000; a few islanders would later report seeing and even speaking with Nakamura, but none reported being assaulted or robbed by the holdout, as residents of Lubang had been during the residency of Lt. Hiro Onoda. Indonesian pilots stationed at the airbase on Morotai would occasionally report spotting clearings and other signs of habitation deep in the jungle, but the rumors went unheeded until 1974.

An Indonesian pilot reported that he had "spotted a naked man, a small hut and what looked like a vegetable field in a clearing some sixty kilometers inland" (JASMW, p. 161). The report reached the Japanese Embassy in Jakarta, and, with the recent emergences of Shoichi Yokoi on Guam and Hiro Onoda on Lubang, the Embassy requested the cooperation the Indonesian government to find out whether this "naked man" was indeed yet another long-lost Japanese holdout. Jakarta assented, and ordered the Morotai airbase to conduct a search.

They knew it was a long shot, and probably very few of them actually expected to find the last Japanese straggler; however, the eleven men sent to check the clearing were duly prepared for what they might encounter. They practiced the Japanese national anthem, Kimigayo, and a few old Japanese army marching songs, "designed to awaken in the listener feeling of patriotism and familiarity." They brought with them a rising-sun flag--the emblem of the Imperial Japanese Army--and a photograph of a geisha. After three days of marching through dense jungle, they found "Nakamura City." There Teruo stood, naked apart from his fundoshi--a Japanese-style loincloth--amazed as Indonesian airmen emerged from the treeline, singing an anthem he had not heard in decades. On December 18th, after thirty years of disbelief, the war was finally over for Private Teruo Nakamura. (JASMW, p. 161)

Nakamura, both because of his Amis ethnicity and his low rank, did not receive a hero's welcome in Japan, as had Lt. Hiro Onoda. As a subject of a former Japanese colony, Nakamura's nationality was put into question. Was he Japanese, or Taiwanese? Should he be repatriated to Japan, or Taiwan? Although he almost certainly perceived himself as Japanese, Teruo Nakamura was repatriated to Taiwan after a short convalescence in Jakarta. Whether he chose to return to Taiwan or was denied entry by the Japanese government is not entirely clear. The ambivalent treatment Teruo Nakamura received from the nation for which he had fought for so long sparked a measure of public outrage in Japan. A group calling itself the Association for the Warm Welcome of Nakamura Terou coalesced, which urged the Japanese government to provide Nakamura with full Japanese citizenship and an adequate pension for his military service. Teruo's recompense for thirty years as a soldier in the Japanese army came out to Y68,000, a paltry sum equivalent to $1,100 USD today.

It is fair to say that Japan was split regarding how to treat Private Nakamura. Some no doubt believed that he and the other Takasago Volunteers were little more than local mercenaries and did not deserved the honor accorded to proper Japanese soldiers. Others were probably compelled to support Nakamura out of a sense of obligation to indigenous people who stood at the front lines of Japan's imperial project. Outfits like the Takasago Volunteers were indispensable to the war effort, both because of their local knowledge and expertise, but also as examples of the benefits of Japanese acculturation. Men like Teruo Nakamura were, in effect, indigenous ambassadors for the Japanese Empire. The guerrilla training they received from their Japanese commanders and the daring missions they undertook were an endorsement of the empire's inclusiveness, and contributed in many ways to the IJA's successes with different indigenous tribes across Asia. Still other Japanese probably perceived Teruo Nakamura as a tragic victim: forced to join a cause that was not his own, regarded as inferior by his Japanese officers, and thoroughly duped into believing that Japan was indestructible. Nakamura would be the first one to contest his characterization as a victim, although he had every reason to be angry and bitter.

Like many other indigenous servicemen, Teruo Nakamura probably felt betrayed by the IJA. He had given his life for Japan, had held nothing back; in return, he received a lukewarm reception and a fistful of dollars. After decades of unwavering service, Teruo was dismissed as little more than a mercenary whose usefulness had worn thin. Although we cannot say exactly how he felt, living out his last years on Taiwan, in the photos taken after his discovery, he looks serious, bitter, and taciturn. Nakamura had been one of thousands of indigenous peoples across Asia who allied with the Japanese and their imperial project, often willingly although sometimes not. Most were seeking an elevation in their status, and were betting and hoping that Japan's imperial ambitions would improve their lives and the lives of their people. Teruo Nakamura "became" Japanese in order to elevate his status in what he believed was to be the new world order: the Greater East Asia Co-Prosperity Sphere. The might of the Imperial Japan was unquestioned in Asia at the time. The Imperial Japanese Army had defeated Russia and China and conquered vast stretches of territory with apparent ease. When Nakamura joined the Takasago Volunteers, he believed firmly that he was joining the winning side, the side which would determine affairs in Asia for years to come. His return was painful: the reward he had expected for his years of service to the Empire had vanished; the Empire itself had turned to dust. He had wagered his entire life on the success of the Empire, and had lost hard.

In the village of Dehegila on Morotai, a monument to Nakamura Teruo stands at a crossroads. A few men of Dehegila can still remember seeing Nakamura while ranging in the jungle, and speaking with him in limited Japanese. They told him the war was over. He told them Japan was invincible. In 1979, Teruo Nakamura, aged 60, died of lung cancer in Taiwan. Nakamura is forever known as the last Japanese holdout, although rumors of more abounded for years after his emergence. He is also the most mysterious of the holdouts. He died just a few short years after leaving Morotai, and he said very little about his experiences or beliefs. Nakamura's motivations will always be matters of speculation, but we should take his words to the men of Dehegila as a fair epitaph: "Japan is invincible."

Sources:

Beatrice Trefalt, Japanese Army Stragglers and Memories of the War in Japan, 1950-75 (Routledge: London, 2003).

"Teruo Nakamura," accessed April 21, 2014, http://en.wikipedia.org/wiki/Teruo_Nakamura.

"Takasago Volunteers," accessed April 21, 2014, http://en.wikipedia.org/wiki/Takasago_Volunteers.

Deanna Ramsey, "Out of the jungle," Jakarta Post, September 21, 2012.

Sergeant Shoichi Yokoi

In 1972, after 27 years of hiding, Sergeant Shoichi Yokoi was discovered deep in the jungles of Guam, the last holdout of the Imperial Japanese Army to be found on the island.

Yokoi was born in 1915 in a small village in Aichi Prefecture located in central Japan. Shoichi never knew his biological father. His mother married another man during her pregnancy, whom she later divorced while Shoichi was still very young. He was ashamed he had no father, and his classmates bullied him for it. After his return to Japan and the accompanying media furor his classmates were interviewed about him. They described him as a quiet child, "nothing special," that he liked to make kites, and was good at geometry. He was "well-behaved and serious" and had been "impatient to enter the army" (JASMW, p. 117). The picture is of an unassuming young man, perhaps somewhat unsure of himself.

As a young man, Shoichi Yokoi supported himself in his home village of Saori as an apprentice tailor, acquiring skills he would later use while on Guam. In 1941, at the age of 26, Yokoi was conscripted into the Imperial Japanese Army. Initially, Sergeant Yokoi was attached to a supply regiment in the occupied territory of Manchuria--or Manchukuo--the main staging area for Japan's invasion of China. As the tides of the Great Pacific War turned against the Empire, however, the IJA transferred tens of thousands of soldiers from its eastern periphery to mount a defense of the Mariana Islands, New Guinea, and the Philippines. Early in 1943, amidst the mounting successes of the Allies' island-hopping campaign, Sgt. Yokoi received orders to transfer to the 38th Regiment in the Mariana Islands. From Manchuria to the Marianas, he traveled thousands of miles inside a packed transport carrier from one unknown country to the next. He arrived on Guam in February 1943, just over a year before the US invasion in June 1944.

Guam is the largest of the Mariana Islands and its central and southern parts were and remain mostly dense jungle. The Battle of Guam was fought mainly on the west coast.

Did Yokoi know the war was over? His first years of military life were in Manchuria, a staging area, but calm and far from any battlefields. According to the account he gave after his discovery and return to Japan, Yokoi was sure by 1952 that the war was over and that Japan had lost. Before he was transferred to Guam as part of the Imperial Army's attempt his time in the military had been uneventful. What compelled him to stay in the jungle for another 20 years? It is likely that Yokoi had never seen combat before the Battle of Guam. He was well-trained, to be sure, diligent, but untested in battle. The US attack was preceded by aerial bombardment tanks-- the Japanese forces on the island were primarily infantry supported by artillery. They had no air support, no tanks, and no means nor plan of escape. By late June 1944, the Japanese Navy had been almost completely decimated in the Battle of the Philippine Sea, called a "turkey shoot" by American pilots, and which saw the sinking of most of Japan's aircraft carriers and support. The Allied campaign in the Marianas started with heavy bombardment from carrier aircraft. 22,000 Japanese soldiers, many of whom, like Sgt. Yokoi, had never seen combat, and others who had seen too much, were trapped on an island of just 200 square miles. The tension in the Japanese ranks must have unimaginable when the Americans finally landed on the morning of July 21.

Sgt. Shoichi Yokoi's unit was stationed in the south of the island in the mountains overlooking Guam's largest freshwater body, Fena Lake. They were located far away from the main Japanese Army force in Agana fighting the force of invading US Marines. They found themselves caught between a well-equipped Marine division invading Agana to the north and a brigade attacking Agat to their south. The Japanese managed to hold off the Marines invading Agat with machine-gun fire and artillery, but the mountains pressed close behind them and they had little room to maneuver. By nightfall July 21, the Americans had taken beachheads around Agat and the Japanese were forced to retreat into the mountains. The Japanese made several failed attempts to recapture the beachheads, mostly at night, and all with heavy losses of men and materiel. By July 25 the Americans had linked their beachheads at Agat and Agana, and Sgt. Shoichi Yokoi and a group of other survivors found themselves cut off from their command structure, thoroughly outnumbered and surrounded by Allied forces. After all those years of calm in a storm, Sgt. Shoichi Yokoi was suddenly closer to the fighting than he had ever been before. In September 1944, Shoichi's mother received notice of her son's death.

Yokoi was not alone during the first two decades of hiding. Until the early 1950s, Sergeant Yokoi was part of a large group of survivors of the Battle of Guam, over twenty in all. After nearly a decade, this original group had been reduced by disease, accidents, and malnutrition to merely seven.

Yokoi maintained a network of dugout caves and other shelters in different locations. He moved periodically between them, and he made sure the entrances were always very well-hidden. Before the last of his comrades died in 1964, he would visit them occasionally, but he preferred to live separately. After his discovery, he showed some of his shelters to officials, who remarked that they were nearly impossible to detect. His primary dwelling, a cave eight feet underground, Shoichi dug out from underneath a bamboo grove. Yokoi chose the site because the roots of bamboo reinforce the soil above and would keep the cave from collapsing. He kept the entrance small and concealed by a set of blinds made of leaves. He constructed a ladder from bamboo to enter the cave. The cave itself was just over three feet high. In it were a kitchen with some implements, a fireplace with a ventilation shaft, and a toilet with a sewage line leading out to a river.

Always mindful of detection, Shoichi remained in his shelters during the day, obscuring his tracks so they would not reveal him. At night he emerged to collect food. The largest animal on Guam is the "carabao," or water buffalo; however, they are only found in the lowlands and are kept by the native Chamorro people. In the early years when there were more men in the group they would occasionally take a carabao, probably because they lacked the skills to collect smaller game. Wild pigs and boars were ubiquitous and not creatures that anyone would ever miss. Yokoi managed to kill a wild boar once: it made him nauseous and he subsequently banned them from his diet.

He described obtaining food as his "constant hardship" during his thirty years on Guam. The search for enough food was certainly a hardship, but it was also a chance for Yokoi to use his tailoring skills and his creativity. He constructed beautiful and ingenious eel traps out of wild reeds. He wove fine nets out of tree bark fibers to catch shrimp and fish. He collected coconuts, mangos, Sago palm nuts, crabs, snails, even birds. He made a boxtrap to catch rats; he liked rat meat, especially the liver. From coconut shells he made an oil-burning lantern. He used coconut milk to cook some of his food. He boiled all of his water. The smoke blackened his utensils and his lungs, but it also kept away lice, mosquitoes, and other insects that carry disease. For 28 years, Shoichi Yokoi avoided illness and infection extremely well. He wrote later of his thoughts during a rare bout of sickness: "No! I cannot die here. I cannot expose my corpse to the enemy. I must go back to my hole to die. I have so far managed to survive but all is coming to nothing now."

However much army indoctrination may have affected the young Shoichi, more important to him still must have been his memories of childhood and adolescence. He tried not to think of his mother growing old alone in Saori. He wrote later, "it was pointless to cause my heart pain by dwelling on such things." The question of why he stayed, knowing the war was over, can only be answered by understanding what home meant to Shoichi Yokoi.

Sergeant Yokoi had nothing to return to: no strong family awaited him in Japan; no promising career; no girlfriend or wife pined for him. He had no great honor to bring back home, no victories to boast of. Japan held nothing for him and he held even less for Japan. He was not driven by ideology. He did not consider himself to be a soldier who was still fighting. He was simply a man trying to survive a hostile environment with no hope of escape. He had left hope behind. It died with his comrades in senseless banzai charges, and the relentless American search-and-destroy missions that decimated the few who had survived them.

"Private Yokoi's War and Life on Guam, 1944-1972," written by Shoichi Yokoi's nephew, Omi Hatashin, is based on interviews with Yokoi and his memoirs of his years in hiding. The book reveals Yokoi not as a die hard soldier, but a man committed to living, even in the absence of hope or reason. "The only thing that gave me the strength and will to survive was my faith in myself," Yokoi said in 1986.

However, on the day he was "discovered" in January 1972, Shoichi Yokoi was finally ready to die. The very last of his comrades had been dead for eight years. He had not spoken to another living soul in that time. Jesus Duenas and Manuel Degracia came across Shoichi deep in the jungle by the Talofofo River around dusk while they were checking their shrimp traps. Yokoi rushed at them, dropping a net full of his own hand-made shrimp traps, and tried to grab one of their rifles. They subdued Shoichi, who was undernourished, though strong for his size. As they led him away at gunpoint, Yokoi begged the two men to kill him. Yokoi did not want to face what he imagined was ahead of him: the fate of a "non-person" in Japanese society. Instead of granting his wish, Duenas and Degracia took Shoichi to Duenas' home, where they gave him some food before bringing him to the local commissioner's office. He explained that although he knew the war over he had been afraid that he would be killed if he came out of hiding.

He returned to Japan an instant celebrity, if not a curiosity. He toured the country, answering endless questions about his years on Guam. Shoichi Yokoi later married and became a TV personality, famous for his advocacy of frugal living. Yokoi taught his viewers about his survival techniques, instructing millions of Japanese how he constructed his eel traps out of reeds. He hearkened back to an era of simplicity and self-sufficiency that Japan had lost in the post-war period. Yokoi was a living reminder of an entire way of being that had been extinguished by war, atomic holocaust and occupation. This reputation, and his playful, charming personality, led him to pursue a career in politics. In 1974, just two years after returning from Guam, Yokoi ran unsuccessfully for Japan's House of Councilors. Over the years, Shoichi Yokoi repeatedly expressed the desire to meet Emperor Hirohito personally, to apologize for his failing as a soldier. He never got to meet the Emperor face-to-face, although while visiting the Imperial Palace he spoke his regret aloud: "I deeply regret that I could not serve you well. The world has certainly changed, but my determination to serve you will never change." His regret at not having the courage to die in battle as his comrades did persisted throughout his life. Like many Japanese war veterans, Yokoi was burdened by a feeling of survivor's guilt. He was never able to reconcile his pre-war social conditioning and his military training with his actions. He was burdened by his own temerity to live.

Shoichi Yokoi should not be remembered as a victim. He was a survivor first, and a victim only of his own shame. He was an ingenious man who never gave up his will to live, despite in his own mind, having no right to live. His shame at having failed tormented him, but it did not drive him to suicide, which would have been the "honorable" thing to do. His code of morality, his perception of his duty, burdened him, but it also may have saved his life. Yokoi had laid himself so low, had destroyed any thought of redemption for himself, that even seppuku, ritual suicide, became impossible for him. Ritual suicide is a redemptive act. Yokoi considered himself so far past any redemption that even to attempt to kill himself would have demanded more dignity than he had left. He no longer considered that he had any right to such a course. To attempt to redeem himself by taking his own life — as quite a few Japanese veterans in fact did after the end of the war — would have added insult to injury. Ritual suicide was reserved for soldiers who had failed, but still had some shred of honor left, enough at least to kill themselves and face atonement in the next life. Shoichi Yokoi had every reason to kill himself, but he did consider himself worthy of such a hallowed act. His shame trapped him on Guam, unable to face the world, but it also saved him from taking his own life.

Recall the observation of the French writer and philosopher Albert Camus that "sometimes it takes more courage to live" than to die. Many thousands of Japanese soldiers chose to die in suicidal charges, or banzai attacks, during the Battle of Guam and elsewhere during the last days of the Great Pacific War. Sgt. Shoichi Yokoi was one of the lucky few to survive, and he chose to keep on living. His reasons may have been misguided or inconsistent, but they were his own. Ultimately, his was the more courageous choice. Shoichi Yokoi, aged 82, died a national hero on September 22, 1997 in Nagoya.

Sources:

Mike Lanchin, "Shoichi Yokoi, the Japanese soldier who held out in Guam," BBC World Service, January 23, 2012, accessed April 1, 2014, http://www.bbc.com/news/magazine-16681636.

Lawrence Cunningham and Janice Beaty, A History of Guam (Bess Press, 2001), 268-69.

"Shoichi Yokoi - Last WWII Straggler on Guam," accessed April 1, 2014, http://ns.gov.gu/scrollapplet/sergeant.html.

Beatrice Trefalt, Japanese Army Stragglers and Memories of the War in Japan, 1950-75 (Routledge: London, 2003).

The New Guinea Stragglers

For some Japanese stragglers the real struggle was neither the war nor their years in hiding, but their return to Japan and their reception at home. The New Guinea stragglers were depicted as weird, oddballs, and "Tarzans." This was a typical response to returning soldiers in Japan in the immediate post-war period as the Japanese government and population sought to distance themselves from the fanatical devotion to Emperor and country that had characterized the war years. Ridiculing the stragglers, remarking on their "strangeness," was a way for the Japanese public to distinguish their own participation in Japan's imperialist war from that of the "fanatics." The decades after the end of the war saw Japanese attitudes towards the stragglers gradually change. From the late 1940s to the early 1970s, the stragglers went from being, in the Japanese public mind, exotic "jungle men" to victims of wartime propaganda and fanaticism and finally, in the case of Hiro Onoda, heroes and exemplars of traditional values.

Two groups of stragglers repatriated from New Guinea in 1950 and 1955 received quite different receptions when they finally returned home. The first group were referred to as "jungle men" by Japanese newspapers, which regaled their audiences with lurid tales of their savage life in the wilderness. The second group were hailed as heroes and the "living spirits of the war dead"; literally, dead men who had come back to life. Over the course of five short years Japanese attitudes towards holdouts changed dramatically. We will review the lives these men lead in the jungles of New Guinea before transitioning to a culture history of post-war Japan in an effort to explain the differing public perceptions of stragglers between 1950, 1955, and beyond.

The stragglers repatriated from New Guinea in 1950 were part of a larger group of Japanese soldiers who had been cut off from their command in late 1943. The men were deployed to the town of Finschafen on New Guinea's eastern Huon Peninsula in March 1942. Japan's campaign in New Guinea was initially quite successful: Australian forces lost control of New Guinea early in the war, retreating from the strategic town of Rabaul on New Guinea's northeastern coast in early 1942. Over the next two years, the Imperial Japanese Army turned Rabaul into a fortress: at the height of the Japanese occupation, more than 100,000 soldiers were stationed in and around the city. Rabual became the headquarters for the Japanese army in the South Pacific, while Finschhafen served as a secondary airbase hub. Finschhafen was strategically important in the eyes of both Japanese and Australian military planners because its position gave it control over the Vitiaz Straight separating New Guinea from New Britain, the gateway to Australian waters.

In September 1943, after a brief period of preparation, Australian forces landed on beaches across New Guinea's northeastern coast. The Japanese forces on New Guinea were under-supplied and lacked firepower equivalent to the Australians. By the time Australian soldiers landed on the Huon Peninsula in late 1943, the Japanese defenders were low on ammunition and morale. Their supply lines were stretched, and they occupied one of the more far-flung Japanese bases during the war. They were removed from any potential aid or support, facing a technologically superior enemy. Japanese commanders on the island exhorted their men to summon their spiritual strength to defeat the well-armed Australians.

The division holding Finschhafen was quickly decimated in the fighting with Australian forces. The Battle of Finschhafen lasted only two months: the Japanese at Finchaffen were unprotected from the Royal Australian Air Force's bombardment—they managed to shoot down only one Australian bomber using a Nambu light-machine gun. Japanese casualties from the initial bombardment were low, but the relentless bombing destroyed their morale and left them paralyzed, paving the way for a pincers movement by the Australian Army's 9th Division.

The exact extent of Japanese casualties during the Huon campaign has never been reliably established, although of the 12,500 soldiers stationed on the peninsula approximately 8,000 were killed in the fighting. About 4,000 soldiers managed to flee west to make their last stand at Sio, which the Australians later captured in March 1944. At Sio, malnutrition and disease took the heaviest toll on the Japanese. Of the 8,000 soldiers which managed to arrive at Sio after the start of the Huon campaign in September 1943, more than half died of starvation and disease before the Australians captured the town in March. The Allied campaign for the Huon Peninsula lasted a total of six months. By March 1944, Australian forces firmly held Rabaul, Lae, Finschhafen, Sio and Madang.

The group of stragglers repatriated in 1950 were the last survivors of the Australian offensive against Finschaffen in September-October 1943. Their resistance in shambles, overwhelmed by Australian tanks, mortars, and aerial attack, the remaining troops Finschhafen and made their way through the dense jungle to Madang. The men were malnourished, suffering fatigue, shock and despair. Yet they were the lucky ones. For five months they marched, vaguely hoping to find relief at Madang, their numbers steadily eroded as men collapsed from exhaustion, succumbed to disease, committed suicide or fell victim to attacks by New Guineans. By the time they neared their destination, Madang had already been captured by the Australians and most of its defenders had been killed. The survivors of Finschhafen had been reduced to merely eight men. They looked down on the Australians occupying Madang from the Finesterre Ridge and knew there would be no rescue, at least not for the moment.

Even then, however, their luck did not desert them. The eight survivors from Finschhafen were captured by New Guinean tribesmen about fifty miles south of Madang: they were taken before the tribal chief who took pity on them and offered them his protection. They lived as members of the village for the next seven years, a lifestyle which contributed to their depiction as exotic "Tarzans" when they were finally repatriated to Japan in February 1950. It is fair to say that without this protection, the men would have succumbed to disease, starvation, or Australian mop-up operations.

The Finschhafen survivors did not consider themselves deserters, stragglers, or holdouts, merely soldiers who had been cut of from their command and whose duty was to survive until they could reunite with their comrades. Surrender was not an acceptable option: not only was surrender unbearably shameful, the men believed that they would be executed in Allied custody. They had been mostly ignorant of the state of the war, unaware the tide was turning decisively against Japan. They had no way of learning of Hiroshima, Nagasaki, or Japan's surrender in September 1945. As far as they knew, Japan's defeats in the South Pacific were nothing but a temporary setback, an isolated case of the enemy getting the upper hand, and the area would eventually be recaptured.

The expected rescue never came. Instead, in late 1949, local police were informed of the presence of Japanese survivors in the remote village. The police arrested them and transferred them to Manus Island, then to Brisbane, and finally to Japan. A photograph taken of the group shows them smiling, wearing uniforms provided by the Red Cross. The welcome they received in Japan was cool, to say the least. They were barely interviewed at the time of their repatriation, so much of the information we have about the first group of New Guinea stragglers comes from a later date. The Japanese newspapers of the time described the group simply as "jungle men," "Tarzans" and "ape-men" part savages, part soldiers deluded by now-denounced Imperial propaganda. The *Mainichi Shimbun* welcomed them home with the headline: "Tarzan lifestyle in the jungle: five years on mice and potatoes," and listed the strange foods the stragglers had eaten — grubs and snakes, for example — and the fact they had only worn loincloths for the last five years. How they survived was considered much more interesting, or at least easier to talk about, then why they persisted in the jungle for so long.

The response of the Japanese media and public to the first group of New Guinea stragglers was greatly affected by the fact that the Occupation was still ongoing. American troops patrolled the streets, war crimes trials were still underway, and the Occupation-imposed censorship controlled the newspapers, radio and public statements by the government. Praising Imperial soldiers for their wartime sacrifice, calling them heroes, was simply not possible in the context of American occupation and censorship. Commemorating the war dead or honoring war heroes would have risked even more censorship and control, and the entire Japanese public at the time seemed to know instinctively that capitulation, shame and regret were the order of the day — at least until the Americans had gone. For this reason the first group of New Guinea stragglers to return received a very cool, even slightly dismissive, reception when they finally arrived home. They were portrayed much differently than Japanese POWs returned from Russia and China, who received sympathetic treatment at home. The warm reception for Japanese POWs was in stark contrast with the official policy of the Imperial Japanese Army, which stated that soldiers who had allowed themselves to be captured were as guilty as deserters, and were to be punished accordingly. The first group of New Guinea stragglers raised questions about the role of ordinary Japanese civilians and soldiers during the war, their measure of guilt for war crimes, and reminded everyone of the honest devotion to the Emperor and the Japanese Empire they had displayed so proudly for years. They were — for the time being — politically embarrassing. POWs, on the other hand, symbolized Japan's capitulation and elicited a public feeling of sympathy. They represented Japan's defeat in plain and simple terms, without the complicated narrative the first group of New Guinea stragglers evoked. It is impossible to say how the Japanese public really felt about the New Guinea stragglers considering that the Japanese media was so heavily censored and influenced by the Occupation authorities.

Japan changed rapidly over the next five years before the discovery and return home of the second group of New Guinea stragglers, so much so that when they were repatriated in 1954 they received a very different kind of homecoming than the 1949 stragglers. The four men were the very last survivors of a forced march made by the remnants of a battalion from Wewak to Hollandia in April 1944. Wewak was then the site of the largest Japanese airbase in New Guinea, the station of the Fourth Air Army. In August 1943, the Royal Australian Air Force undertook a massive bombing campaign to put the Wewak airbase out of commission, which largely succeeded. In five days the RAAF destroyed 100 of the 130 operational aircraft stationed at the Wewak airbase, many of them state-of-the-art fighters that were to be the spearhead of Japan's New Guinea campaign. Even before the devastating August raids, the Fourth Air Army was at half its operational strength because of disease—malaria, diarrhea and yellow fever—and a chronic shortage of spare parts. Over the next year the Wewak battalion was slowly whittled down to barely a few platoons. In April 1944, the remainder of the Fourth Air Army set out on a 200-mile forced march to the strategically vital Japanese base at Hollandia in advance of a massive Allied attack. They never made it to Hollandia. Of the 89 men who left Wewak on April 10, 1944, only 4 survived. Nearly thirty of the men drowned while attempting a river crossing during a monsoon. Many more died of hunger and disease, or fell prey to New Guinea's poisonous wildlife. The group was reduced to 21 men. As they were nearing the town of Vanimo, still some forty miles from Hollandia, they learned their destination, and the last significant Japanese airbase in the South Pacific, had been overrun by the Allies. In mid-June they elected to hide in the jungle and bide their time until Japanese force retook the area. They set up camp and awaited the arrival of reinforcements. Unaccustomed to jungle survival, they survived by pilfering rations from nearby enemy bases. The Allies tracked them back to their camp and attacked, killing most of them. Five men managed to escape, fleeing deeper into the jungle. They cleared some land and attempted to grow crops, which proved very challenging. The five men survived mainly on wild pigs, supplementing pork with lizards, snakes, even caterpillars. All of the men were suffering serious salt deficiency; in 1947, the group was reduced to four after one man succumbed to malaria.

In 1951, after seven years in hiding, the group was discovered. A New Guinean man from a nearby village came across the stragglers while he was hunting. After some initial distrust, the stragglers and the villagers began regular contact. The villagers tried to tell the stragglers that Japan and America were now "friends" and that the Emperor was still alive. The stragglers, however, could not understand that the war was over—the villagers were not making sense. Despite this basic misunderstanding between them, the villagers made periodic visits to the stragglers' camp, and the stragglers in turn visited the village. For three years these friendly relations persisted. In 1954, however, the villagers brought a detachment of police along on one of their visits, and the stragglers were taken into custody. It finally dawned on the men that the war was really over.

On the outside the stories of the two groups are quite similar. All were survivors of calamitous defeats that cut them off from their command structure, and neither had any knowledge of Japan's surrender in September 1945, apart from the word of villagers who might not have had a full picture of the war. None of the men considered themselves deserters: they were following orders to survive and await rescue. Such was the faith both groups had in their comrades' return and Japan's eventual victory that they survived in a hostile and unfamiliar environment with no support for seven and ten years, respectively. Surrender was unthinkable to them, even though both had the option. Considering the many similarities between the two groups of stragglers, it is striking how differently they were received in the public imagination upon their return to Japan.

The first group, repatriated in 1950 while Japan was still under American occupation, were referred to as "strange" by the Japanese media, which focused on the lurid details of their "jungle life." They were a curiosity, interesting for their strange diet and minimal clothing (they had worn only loincloths), not their dedication or resolve, which would have been a delicate subject to raise while American soldiers still patrolled the streets of Japan's ruined cities. By the time the Hollandia group were repatriated in 1954 the situation in Japan had changed radically. The reception the Hollandia group received reflected an emerging public consensus on the war and Japan's responsibility, unshadowed by Occupation, a consensus which has in large part persisted to this day.

The 1954 New Guinea stragglers were received with much greater respect than their 1950 predecessors. Immediately after their return they were taken on a whirlwind tour of Japan, interviewed by the press in cities across the country. As a result, three collapsed from exhaustion—they had barely been given time to recover from their ordeal. The public was fascinated by their story, how they survived, but not in the same way as the 1950 stragglers. The 1950 stragglers were dehumanized by the media, called "jungle men," "Tarzans," "exotic" and so forth. The fact that they survived for years without aid in the jungle was not impressive: it was to be expected since the men had—in their portrayal by the media, at least—regressed to a primitive state. They were essentially depicted as animals. The 1954 stragglers, on the other hand, were pressed on all sides with questions about their survival methods, although for the most part refrained from characterizing their refusal to surrender as heroic resolve. They received hundreds of letters congratulating them on their return, as well as many others asking about sons and brothers still missing in action. Several of the unmarried members of 1954 group received marriage proposals in the mail. Their story was a redemption of Japan's disastrous wartime losses, proof that despite defeat and humiliation Japan still had sons of whom they could be proud. Accordingly, Japanese newspapers referred to the 1954 stragglers by a term that both honored and dehumanized: they were called "living spirits of the war dead." They were reminders of the dead; they were ghosts.

In the public mind, the 1954 stragglers represented the spirit of sacrifice and patriotism embodied during the war. With the US Occupation over, the Japanese public felt much more comfortable expressing their solidarity with war veterans, although they did not embrace stragglers as heroes. A few Japanese newspapers received letters-to-the-editor urging that the planned war shrine at Chidorigafuchi be dedicated to "martyrs of the nation," a term of extreme patriotism, rather than the proposed "unknown victims," which carried no connotation of heroism. They were to be remembered neutrally: not as fallen war heroes, but as anonymous "victims" of the war, and, by extension, war propaganda and Japanese militarism. This characterization of Japanese soldiers as victims, both of the war and of an ungrateful nation that had lost its way, gradually cemented during the 1950s as Japan slowly recovered. Stragglers became, in the public mind, stark reminders of Japan's descent into materialism and the loss of values of honor, loyalty and patriotism. This perception had nothing to do with the actions of the stragglers themselves. From the jungles of New Guinea to Guam, Lubang to Saipan, stragglers emerged over the post-war decades, and each new straggler that returned brought the unanswered questions of the war back into the public mind. Were they heroes? Patriots? Or were they simply deluded by militarist propaganda and Japan's imperial ambitions? By the 1950s, the prevailing opinion on war veterans, and stragglers especially, was that they had been misled by an irrational and cruel wartime government—they had been duped.

In 1960, six years after the last group of New Guinea stragglers returned, two more stragglers were discovered on Guam. They were portrayed as soldiers, certainly, but also as victims. They were applauded for their ingenuity and resolve, but also pitied as the unwitting tools of foolish imperialism.

By the time Shoichi Yokoi and Hiroo Onoda were found in 1972 and 1975, respectively, the perception of soldiers as victims had solidified in the public consciousness. Yokoi, especially, personified the straggler-as-victim. Arriving in Japan after nearly thirty years hiding in the highlands of Guam, he famously told the press, "It is with great embarrassment, but I have returned alive." Yokoi may have been making a joke at the expense of General Douglas MacArthur, who grandly promised "I shall return" after he ordered American forces to retreat from the Philippines. Nevertheless, over the years he repeatedly expressed shame that he had failed his duty to Emperor. Yokoi requested an audience with the Emperor to surrender his rusted rifle — which, as all Japanese soldiers had been told, was a gift from the Emperor — and to apologize personally for not dying in battle. Yokoi characterized the essential Japanese dilemma in the postwar period: whether they were to be proud or ashamed of their participation in the war.

Yokoi's strong desire to make amends for his so-called failure compounded his victim image in the Japanese public mind. Not only was he a victim of war, catastrophic defeat and thirty years in the jungle, Yokoi was a victim of propaganda and ideological indoctrination that taught him to be ashamed of having lived. Yokoi's return coincided with the maturation of the first post-war generation: the first Japanese men and women who had no personal experience of the war or its aftermath. Shoichi Yokoi seemed entirely bizarre to this new generation. They were separated by a vast gulf of time and experience from the conditions that produced Yokoi and guided his actions. They could fathom the system of belief that made him prefer a solitary life in the jungle to the "shame" of return. They were taught that the people and the Emperor had been duped by vain militarists, led astray by imperialist propaganda. It was, in a sense, evasion. Japan's relationship to its "war guilt" has always been a complicated one, mixing denial, stubborn pride, acceptance and shame. The various interpretations of the stragglers over the decades reflect Japan's changing relationship to its "war guilt," and each time a straggler emerged from the jungle, Japanese were given the chance to reflect on the meaning of the war and its antecedents.

Hiroo Onoda, who returned from Lubang in 1975, bucked the trend of victimizing stragglers and other war veterans. He scoffed at the portrayal of Japanese soldiers and civilians who participated in the war effort as the deluded victims of jingoistic propaganda. He was a soldier, Onoda told his interviewers, and a soldier does his duty until he dies or is relieved. He made no excuses either to his Emperor or to his countrymen. He made no apology for either his refusal to surrender or his failure to complete his mission. For decades he refused to express any regret; much later in life, however, Onoda made an apology to the people of Lubang, over thirty of whom died over the course of his one-man guerrilla war.

Onoda's refusal to be cast as a victim reflected the ambiguous feelings many Japanese had about the war. Many recalled their participation in Japan's imperial project quite fondly, as a time of united purpose, national spirit and fierce resolve. Many saw the war as a revival of Japan's premodern feudal values of *bushido* – the warrior code of the samurai – and *ganbaru* – absolute dedication to a goal, however difficult, until it is accomplished. For many Japanese who lived through the war, either as civilians or soldiers, the stragglers, and particularly the unapologetic Onoda, came to represent values that Japan had lost in the decades after the war: unwavering commitment and dedication no matter the odds or the cost. Perhaps the reason the stragglers continue to inspire such interest is that each one represents a different perception of the war: some are mournful, some are bitter, and others remain indignant to this day. The stragglers cover the gamut of emotions inspired by the war and its aftermath, by feudal and modern Japanese society.

Printed in Great Britain
by Amazon

41475369R00066